Anyone f

written by Diana Freeman

1

If you want to learn to play tennis, you must master the skills.
The right equipment is important:

- Your racket must be the correct size and weight for you.
- Wear comfortable sports shoes that support your feet.
- Tennis clothes should be light sports gear.
- You might need a hat, cap or visor for protection from the sun.

Try hitting a ball against a wall until you can control your shots. It's a good idea to go to coaching classes with a group of your own ability. You'll learn to hold your racket properly and to serve the ball. Serving takes lots of practice because it's a very important part of the game.

You can use forehand or backhand strokes to hit the ball, depending where you are on the court. You can play close to the net, or near the back line of the court.

Tennis can be played as "singles" or "doubles". It is played on a rectangular court, marked with lines for singles or doubles play, and divided in the middle by a net. The court may be marked on grass, clay or hard surfaces. It's important to notice the lines and remember which ones to use, depending on whether you are playing singles or doubles.

Singles has two players competing against each other, one at each end of the court. Doubles is played by four people – that is, one pair at each end of the court, playing against each other. Doubles can be "mixed", with a man and a woman in each pair.

The umpire

Important matches need an umpire, who sits on a high seat looking down on the court to judge if a ball is in or out. If he calls "Out!" the players must obey his judgement. He also calls the score, so that the players know who is winning. When a player serves but the ball goes out, the umpire calls "Fault!" and the server has a second try.

If the call is "Love – 15", it means that the serving player has no point, and the receiving player has fifteen points. "Love" always means no point for that player.

When a ball is hit to and fro between players, it's called a rally, which is also the way of beginning a proper tennis game. The winner of a rally is the player who serves first.

Try to watch good players on television or at your local tennis club. You can learn from the way they move, how they reach for difficult shots, and how they move their feet.

You can also learn the scoring by following a game closely.

Scoring

3   **30**

2   **40**

Tennis is played in almost every country in the world. The rules are always the same. You will need to learn words like deuce, lob, sets and tie-breaker.

The scoring system is unusual: love, fifteen, thirty, forty. If both players reach forty points it is called "deuce", then the next point is "advantage" and finally "game". The score of the server is always called first.

Etiquette

At the end of a game, players run to the net and shake hands across it. This is the etiquette of the game – players should always thank each other, no matter who has won. They should thank the umpire, too.

If you don't have an umpire, the server should call the score clearly, always giving the opponent the benefit of any doubt.

Club play

The best way to learn tennis is to play it, and with practice you will improve your game. Join a tennis club and take part in its competitions. There could be opportunities to play at other clubs and in local tennis tournaments. That's all good experience, and you will meet other beginning players too.

On television you can watch many wonderful tennis events around the world. Perhaps one day you could even go to see the world's top players in one of the four most famous tournaments played every year:

- Wimbledon at London in England
- Australian Open at Melbourne in Australia
- French Open at Paris in France
- US Open at New York in USA.

These events are called the Grand Slam tournaments, where professional players compete to win trophies, world rankings and prize money.

Tennis is enjoyed by millions of players of all ages, even some in wheelchairs! It is an Olympic sport – a game worth learning. You can enjoy games with friends, keep fit, and also follow your interest in this popular sport all your life.